The *Midnight Fairy*

CRAFT AND PARTY BOOK

The *Midnight Fairy*
CRAFT AND PARTY BOOK

Sterling Publishing Co., Inc.
New York

Library of Congress Cataoging-in-Publication Data Available

10 9 8 7 6 5 4 3 2 1

Published in 2001 by Sterling Publishing Co., Inc.
387 Park Avenue South, New York, NY 10016

First published in Australia and New Zealand in 1999 by
Tracy Marsh Publications Pty Ltd.
PO Box 116, Henley Beach, SA 5022

© 1999 Tracy Marsh Publications Pty Ltd.

Distributed in Canada by Sterling Publishing
c/o Canadian Manda Group, One Atlantic Avenue, Suite 105
Toronto, Ontario, Canada M6K 3E7

Every effort has been made to ensure that all the information in
this book is accurate. However, due to differing conditions, and
individual skills, the publisher cannot be responsible for any
injuries, losses, and other damages, which may result from the use
of the information in this book.

Printed in China

Sterling ISBN 0-8069-4319-X

ONTENTS

The Song of the
Midnight Fairy

In a grassy glade
when the moon shines bright
a soft sweet scent
fills up the night.
It is the Moon Flower
white and rare
whose perfume wafts
across the air.
Its flowers are striped
with palest green;
its heart-shaped leaves
have a starry gleam.

There the Midnight Fairy
with silken wings
to the flutter of moths
in fine voice sings
while the fairies dance
on the moss below
by the gentle light
of the stars aglow.
And when day comes
she flies away
to her gossamer hammock
and there she'll stay
until the moon
opens up its flower
then she'll come once more
to her fairy bower.

The Midnight fairy

9

Fairy Doll

"The Midnight Fairy is the prettiest fairy you could ever imagine. Her hair is the softest golden color of a summer sunrise. She seems to glow with the light of many stars, and her eyes are twinkling and kind."

The Midnight Fairy Doll is soft bodied with a lycra outer, giving her a silky texture. She has pretty embroidered face features and her luxurious organza dress is stitched onto her body, eliminating any difficult sewing techniques.

MATERIALS

- template plastic or thin cardboard
- scissors
- fabric marking pen
- 19 ¾ in (50cm) of muslin (calico)
- polyester stuffing
- wadding (batting)
- pins
- needle and thread
- 19 ¾ in (50cm) of flesh colored lycra
- dressmaker's carbon
- stranded embroidery thread: pink, blue, brown
- dollmaker's needle or long darning needle
- rouge
- synthetic hair
- 19 ¾ in (50cm) of dark blue organza
- 8 in (20cm) of light blue organza
- gold machine thread
- 2 ⅜ in (6cm) of gold cord

Trace the patterns on page 19 onto the template plastic or cardboard. Cut out the head piece only and leave the rest aside.

Using the fabric marking pen trace the head piece onto the muslin (calico). Before cutting out the head sew around the drawn line with a small machine stitch, or a stretch straight stitch. This makes the seams strong. Leave open where marked. Leaving a small seam allowance cut out the head.

Snip into the curves and turn right way out. Stuff the head and neck very firmly, using a small screwdriver or crochet hook to push the stuffing down.

Cut a 10 in (25cm) square of wadding. Place a small amount of polyester stuffing into the center of the square and roll from corner to corner. Place this roll around the lower part of the head and pin in place just behind the head side seam. Stitch in place. Cut a piece of wadding 8 in (20cm) square and roll in the same fashion. Place this across the top portion of the head that is still exposed. Pin and stitch in place.

Trim away the excess wadding at the back of the head.
Cut another piece of wadding 8 in (20cm) square and place it over the front of the head pulling it to the back and pinning in place to cover the whole head. Stitch in place and trim away excess.

Cut a piece of lycra 8 in (20cm) square. Hold one corner under the front neck edge and pull the rest over to the back of the head. Pin tightly. Hand stitch down the back of the head securely.

Cut a 1 in (2.5cm) square of lycra. Stitch a gathering stitch around the four sides and pull up. Place a small piece of polyester stuffing into the center and pull up tightly. Stitch to secure. Stitch the "nose" onto the face.

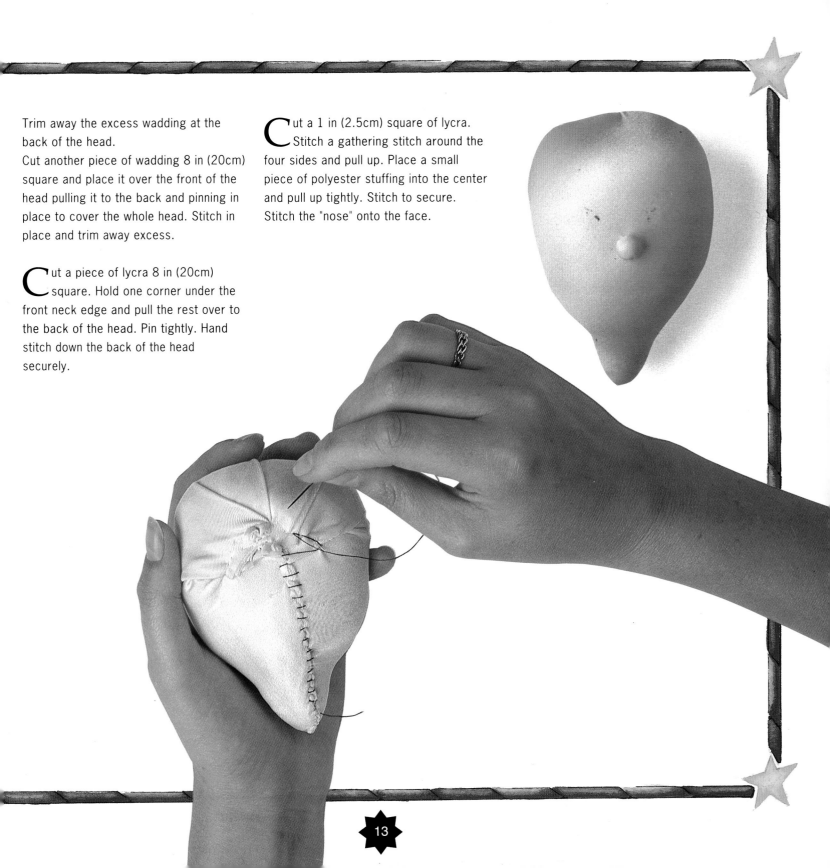

Cut a piece of lycra and a piece of muslin (calico) 16 x 19 3/4 in (40 x 50cm). Fold each in half to measure 16 x 10in (40 x 25cm). Cut out the other pattern pieces from the template plastic and trace around each one onto the folded muslin (calico), except the soles. Position the folded piece of lycra inside the folded piece of muslin (calico), with the folds aligned. Sew a small machine stitch around each of the drawn pieces, leaving open where marked. Cut out each piece leaving a small seam allowance, clip the curves where needed.

Turn both arms and the body piece right way out. There will be muslin (calico) on the inside and lycra on the outside.

Lay a small piece of muslin (calico) over a piece of lycra and trace around the sole pattern twice.
Stitch around the pieces with a small stitch and cut out. Pin these in place, with the muslin (calico) on the outside, onto the foot of each leg and sew in place. Turn right way out.

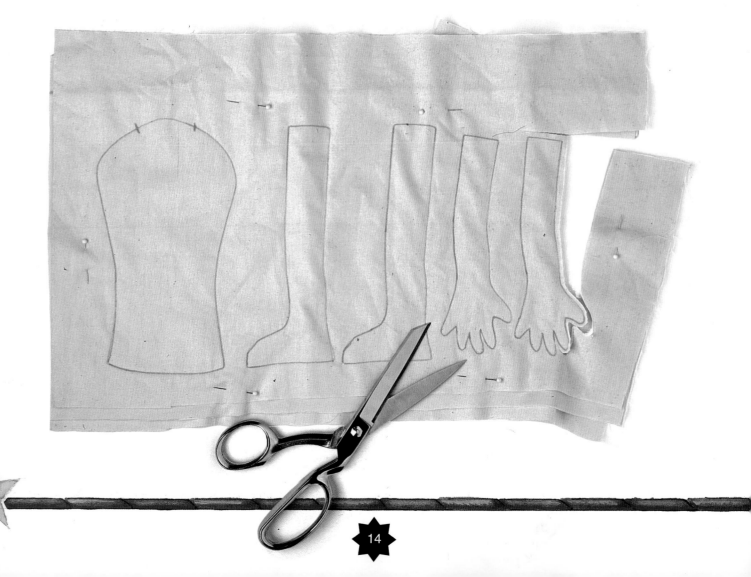

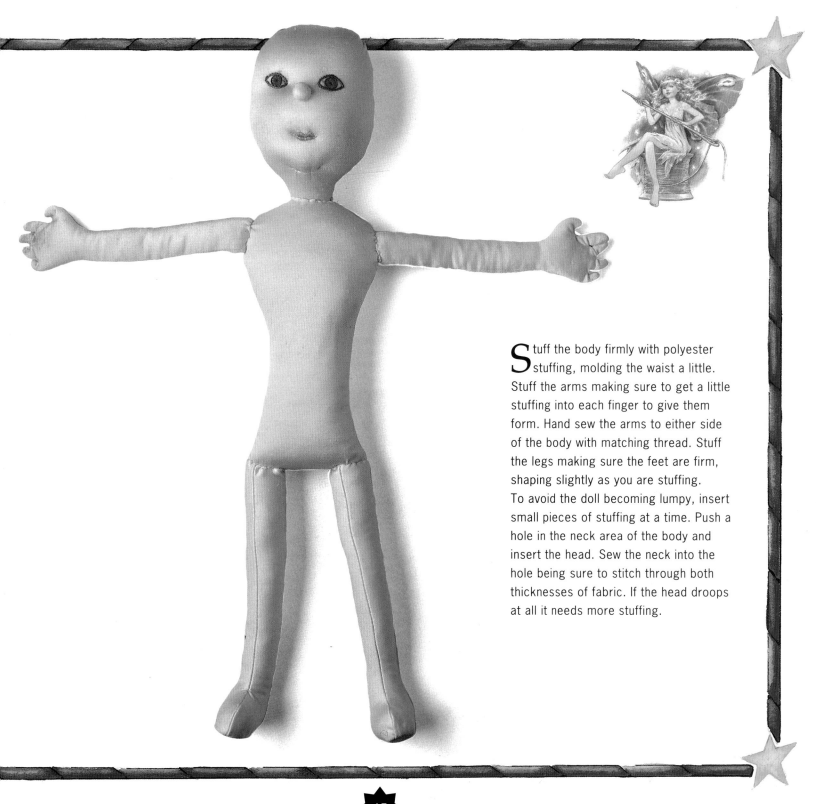

Stuff the body firmly with polyester stuffing, molding the waist a little. Stuff the arms making sure to get a little stuffing into each finger to give them form. Hand sew the arms to either side of the body with matching thread. Stuff the legs making sure the feet are firm, shaping slightly as you are stuffing.

To avoid the doll becoming lumpy, insert small pieces of stuffing at a time. Push a hole in the neck area of the body and insert the head. Sew the neck into the hole being sure to stitch through both thicknesses of fabric. If the head droops at all it needs more stuffing.

Trace the eyes and mouth from the photograph. Use the dressmaker's carbon to transfer the details to the face. Using the dollmaker's needle place a ³⁄₈ in (10mm) stitch where the mouth is to be, to create an indent. Insert the threaded needle from the back to the front of the head, and to the back again, pull firmly and fasten off. Embroider the eyes and mouth using blanket stitch and outline the eyes in stem stitch. Lightly brush rouge onto each cheek.

Remove the lengths of synthetic hair from the package and lay flat, spread to a depth of 4 in (10cm). Machine stitch across the center. Position onto the doll, aligning the stitching to the center of the head. Hand stitch in place. Arrange the hair around the doll's face and trim some short bangs.

The dress is fashioned and stitched onto the doll. Cut one strip of pale blue and one of dark blue organza 8 in (20cm) wide and the length of the fabric. Using the gold thread machine stitch a rolled hem along the long edges of each piece. Cut four 16 in (40cm) lengths from each strip, stitch a gold rolled hem along the cut edges. Place two dark blue pieces over two light blue pieces and gather along a 16 in (40cm) length. Stitch this to the waist, placing the opening to the back. Position and gather the other four pieces in the same way and wrap around the doll's waist, meeting at the front this time. Stitch in place. Stitch small gold star-shaped sequins onto the front of the skirt pieces.

Cut a piece of dark blue organza 10 x 10 in (25 x 25cm). Fold it diagonally from corner to corner. Hand stitch the gold cord into either side of the fold, inserting each end $3/8$ in (10mm). Place over the doll's head and drape to the waist, resembling the photograph. Pin in place and sew by hand to secure. Trim off the excess fabric across the waist-line. Cut a 8 x 2 in (20cm x 5cm) piece of dark blue organza. Fold in half lengthwise and wrap around the waist, covering the raw edges of the other pieces. Hand stitch in place.

MATERIALS
- covered wire
- 12 in (30cm) of white organza
- acrylic paints: blue, mauve
- brush
- glitter paint
- cotton tape
- green florist's tape
- assorted small silk flowers
- cardboard
- wooden skewer
- gold paint
- glitter
- 2 star-shaped crystal jewels
- gold beads

Twist a few 12 in (30cm) lengths of wire together and form a circle to fit the doll's head. Cover the circle of wire with green florist's tape and wire on the small flowers.

Cut two star shapes, using the pattern on page 25, from cardboard. Place a skewer between the two stars and glue to hold. Spray gold. Outline the star shape with glitter paint and glue the star-shaped jewel to the center.

To make the necklace thread gold beads and a crystal star onto the gold thread and tie around the neck to cover the seam between the head and body.

Use these shapes as the pattern for the fairy's wings. Shape two of each size from the covered wire, leaving 1 5/8 in (4cm) protruding from each Cut two pieces of the white organza 3/4 in (2cm) larger than each shape. Position the wire shape between the two pieces. Set the machine to a zig-zag slightly larger than the diameter of the wire and stitch around the shape over the wire.

Trim the organza back to the outside edge of the wire. Repeat for each wing shape.

Refering to the photograph paint the wings with watery blue and mauve paint. Allow to dry and apply the glitter paint around the edges. Brush a fine layer over the body of the wings also. Wind the protruding wires of the four wings together to create a pair of wings and wrap with cotton tape. Stitch to the back of the fairy doll.

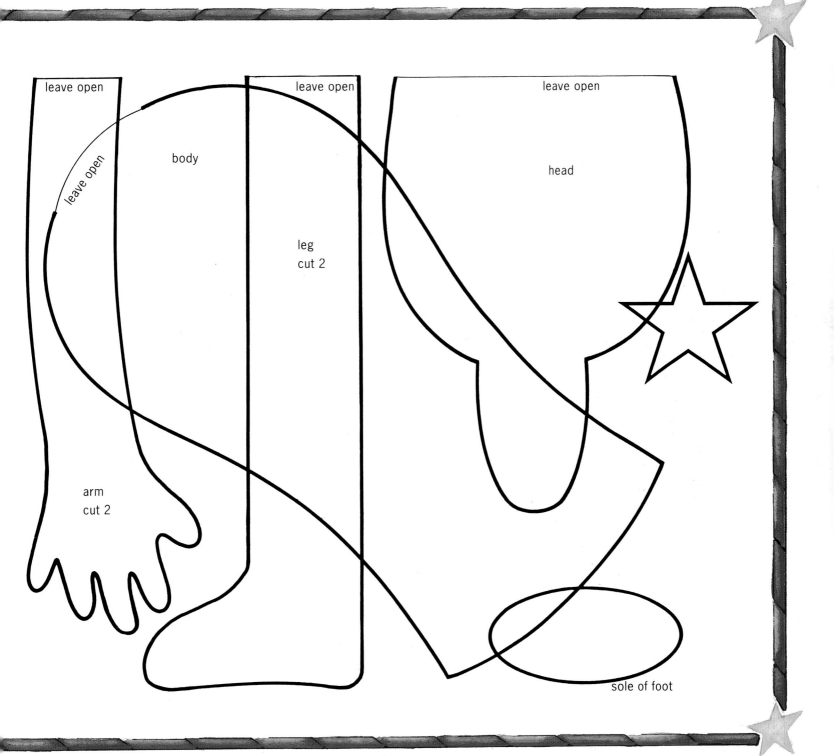

leave open

leave open

leave open

leave open

body

head

leave open

leg
cut 2

arm
cut 2

sole of foot

Castle

*"A fairy bower is beautiful beyond words.
Imagine this splendid castle in a valley near a silver
river which shines brightly in the moonlight."*

The Midnight Fairy's splendid castle
is made from cardboard towers that are covered
in sifted sand which is then sprayed gold.
The addition of delicate foliage and tiny fairies
at the base adds to the magical feel.

MATERIALS

- tracing paper
- pencil
- carbon paper
- firm cardboard
- scissors
- ruler
- craft glue
- 1⅝ in (4cm) diameter cardboard cylinder–8 in (20cm) long
- spray adhesive
- sieve
- sand
- gold spray paint
- 7 in (18cm) diameter round balsa box
- blue acrylic paint
- brush
- music box mechanism
- dried flowers and leaves
- dried grapevine tendrils
- dried moss
- gloss varnish
- small stars and glitter
- small toys and objects for decoration

Trace the pattern pieces on page 25 and transfer to the firm cardboard. Ask an adult to help you cut out the pieces.

Trace the diameter of the lid onto a piece of cardboard and cut out. Glue the main tower to the center of this base. Glue the low tower pieces together, gluing the B pieces to the outer edges. Glue the low tower to the main tower. Cut out the window. Apply glue to the back of the window and position half way up the main tower, hold till secure.

Cut the piece for the main roof, score along the marked lines and glue in place on the top of the cylinder. Measure the height of the main tower and cut a 90 degree segment from the cylinder to this height. Glue to the side of the main tower. Apply glue along the cut edges and position against the side of the main tower, apply pressure until it's secured. Cut and score four spires and glue the seams together. Glue to the castle refering to the photograph for position. Cut and score the spire rooves and glue in place.

Cut the cardboard base back closer to the towers. Ask an adult to spray the entire castle with spray adhesive and dust with an even layer of sifted sand. Allow to dry and apply gold spray paint. Do not use spray paint without an adult's help.

Apply two coats of blue paint to the base and lid of the box.

Drill a hole in the bottom of the box, insert the music box mechanism, with the turntable protruding from the bottom of the box and glue to secure.

Glue the castle onto the lid.

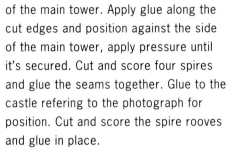

Decorate the base of the castle with dried leaves and flowers. Ask an adult to spray the grapevine tendrils gold. Allow to dry and glue in place. Glue the dried moss up the side of the tower.

Arrange whatever small toys and objects you can find on the base of the castle to create a fairy scene.

Glue the stars and glitter around the base of the box. Ask an adult to apply two coats of varnish to the box base and lid, covering the flower and leaves also. Allow to dry completely between each coat.

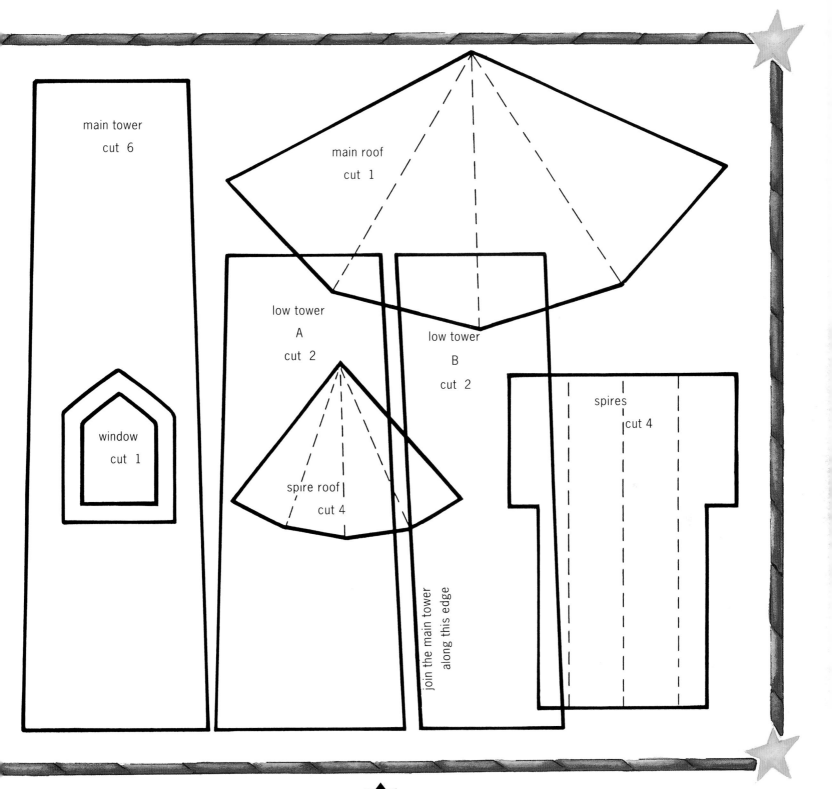

main tower
cut 6

main roof
cut 1

low tower
A
cut 2

low tower
B
cut 2

spires
cut 4

window
cut 1

spire roof
cut 4

join the main tower
along this edge

Wand and Frame

"Have you ever felt the power of a wand being waved?"

Bring the enchantment of fairies to your
bedroom by displaying the glittering wand and
frame on your dressing table. They have been
decorated with pretty jewels
and sparkling glitter.

MATERIALS

- wooden frame (or make your own from cardboard)
- gold spray paint
- glitter
- glitter paint: crystal, purple
- craft glue
- assorted colored crystal jewels

Use a wooden frame or make your own from cardboard.
Ask an adult to spray the frame gold and sprinkle with glitter while still wet.

Apply a line of crystal glitter around the oval opening, with a bow at the bottom. Apply a line of purple glitter around the outer edge.
Position the crystal jewels around the frame where desired. When they look "balanced", glue them down one by one by smearing the back of each jewel with glue and pressing back into place.

MATERIALS

- tracing paper
- pencil
- carbon paper
- thin cardboard
- scissors
- long wooden skewer
- 5 pearls
- 5 triangular mirrors
- oval crystal jewel
- gold spray paint
- glitter paint: dark mauve, light mauve
- craft glue

Trace the star pattern and transfer to the cardboard. Cut out two stars. Glue the stars together with the skewer secured between.

Ask an adult to spray the wand and star gold. Apply the dark mauve glitter paint around the edge. Apply a line of light mauve ⅛ in (5mm) in from the outside edge. Glue the triangular beads into each point of the star, and glue the pearls above each one. Glue the crystal oval onto the center of the star, and place dots of dark mauve around it.

Stardust Bag

"The Midnight Fairy will send a dream moth to sprinkle silver stardust on your eyes and so fill your night's sleep with dreams."

The Stardust Bag is made from glamorous velvet and lamé. You can use it to hold jewelry or any other secret treasures!

U se either a 12 in (30cm) plate or compass to draw a circle onto the wrong side of the velvet and the wrong side of the lamé. Cut out the circles and place right sides together. Pin to hold. Sew around the circles, 3/8 in (10mm) from the raw edge. Leave a 4 in (10cm) section open. Turn right sides out.

Cut 4

F old twice to find the center and insert
the plastic or cardboard circle aligned
with the center. Pin around the edge of
the plastic to hold in place. Machine stitch
around the edge of the circle.
Hand stitch the opening closed with
small even stitches.

U sing the gold thread, stitch buttonholes around the circle, 1⅝ in
(4cm) from the edge. Place them 2 in
(5cm) apart. Thread the gold cord
through the buttonholes. Following the
manufacturer's instructions apply the
double-sided adhesive to a 10 in (25cm)
square of lamé fabric. Trace the star pattern on page 32 and transfer the four
star shapes onto the paper backing. Cut
out and peel off the backing. Place two
stars against each other, positioning one
end of the gold cord between them, and
press to adhere; repeat with the other
two stars and the other end of the cord.
Pull gently and evenly on the gold cords
to draw the circle of fabric up into a
"bag". Evenly distributing the cord
through the buttonholes.

Paper Tole

*"The Midnight Fairy has such grace
and splendor that seeing her will almost
stop your breath."*

Paper tole is the art of creating a 3-D image from flat pictures. With some careful work, you can create a beautiful fairy paper tole.

MATERIALS

- 6 prints*
- pencil
- craft knife or scissors
- spare blades
- matte spray
- shaping tool
- long-nosed tweezers
- brown felt-tip pen
- silicone glue
- high glaze
- fine paint brush
- cutting mat (optional)
- vinyl placemat
- craft glue
- fine clear glitter

The print needed to make the paper-tole project can be found in the back of the book beginning on *page 141. Make color copies of the print with a scanner or copier. You will need 6 prints in total. Plus, copy an extra print for the project on page 60. Mark each print so they do not become mixed up. Mark them: base, 1, 2, 3, 4, and 5. Ask an adult to spray each print with two coats of matte spray; this will enable you to cut and shape your pieces without causing damage.

Color photocopy the illustrations over the next three pages and cut the needed pieces from each print.

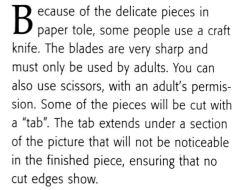

Because of the delicate pieces in paper tole, some people use a craft knife. The blades are very sharp and must only be used by adults. You can also use scissors, with an adult's permission. Some of the pieces will be cut with a "tab". The tab extends under a section of the picture that will not be noticeable in the finished piece, ensuring that no cut edges show.

Carefully lift off your cut pieces and keep them in the correct groups.

Each piece will need shaping. This will depend on the shape of the piece and where it is to be positioned. Look closely at the photograph on page 35 to help with this. Either lay the pieces on the vinyl placemat, or hold in your hand, and rub the shaping tool over them.

The cutout pieces are numbered in sequence according to how you should apply them to the base print. The dabs of silicone need to be applied in varying heights to help achieve the depth of field. Again, refer to the photograph for indication of the height needed in each place. When applying the cut pieces do not push the piece down or you will flatten the silicone dab. Silicone glue must only be used by an adult. Following the illustrations, cut out the pieces shown from each print. Shape and apply the cut pieces according to the order indicated by the numbers alongside each piece.

Print 1

3
2
4
5
6
1

37

Print 2

16

12

13

8

21

9

10

11

7

Print 3

14

15

18

Print 4

17

19

20

22

27

25

Print 5

Five flowers 23
All stars 24

39

Fairy Tale Book

"When the moon shines bright the Midnight Fairy sits in a tall tree above her castle, laughing with delight while she watches the fairies dance below."

Create a delicate scene in an old book by cutting away a frame and building a landscape with papier mâché. Decorate with dried flowers, nuts and grapevine tendrils. Lots of rich gold and sparkling glitter give a magical look.

There the Midnight Fairy

with silken wings

to the flutter of moths

in fine voice sings

While the fairies dance

on the moss below

by the gentle light

of the stars aglow

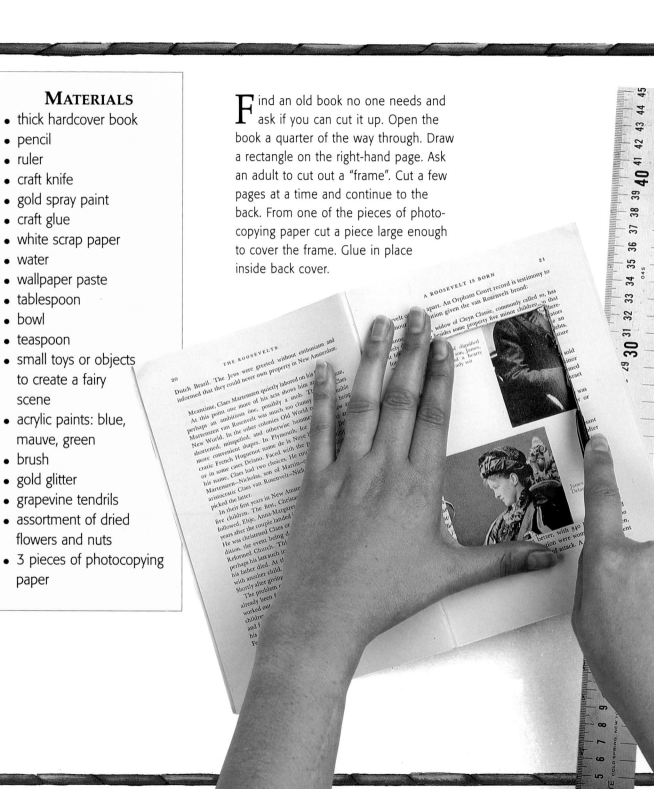

MATERIALS
- thick hardcover book
- pencil
- ruler
- craft knife
- gold spray paint
- craft glue
- white scrap paper
- water
- wallpaper paste
- tablespoon
- bowl
- teaspoon
- small toys or objects to create a fairy scene
- acrylic paints: blue, mauve, green
- brush
- gold glitter
- grapevine tendrils
- assortment of dried flowers and nuts
- 3 pieces of photocopying paper

F ind an old book no one needs and ask if you can cut it up. Open the book a quarter of the way through. Draw a rectangle on the right-hand page. Ask an adult to cut out a "frame". Cut a few pages at a time and continue to the back. From one of the pieces of photocopying paper cut a piece large enough to cover the frame. Glue in place inside back cover.

Ask an adult to spray the entire book gold, both the cover and the open pages. The spray paint will "glue" the pages. If not, apply some craft glue between the pages to keep them in place. Make a papier mâché pulp by mixing together one cup of water, torn paper, and two tablespoons of wallpaper paste. Use the teaspoon to shape the pulp into a landscape around the sides of the "frame".

Build up across the bottom and left-hand edge. Model a mountain shape in the center of the background. Use the back of the teaspoon as a modeling tool. Allow the pulp to dry. Use small toys or objects to create a fairy scene.

43

Cut two pieces of photocopying paper to the same size as the book pages. Photocopy the poem adjacent onto one of these. Ask an adult to lightly spray gold around the edges of the page. Glue the poem to the left-hand page of the book. Curl up the corners of the page.

Draw a rectangle in the center of the other page a little smaller than the frame and tear a jagged opening. Ask an adult to spray gold. Glue the page to the right-hand side of the book, aligning the opening over the frame. Use the craft glue to apply the remaining flowers, grapevine tendrils, and nuts to the book. Position and glue around the frame and down the center. Glue small stars on. Glue a few small stars inside the scene onto the sky area.

There the Midnight Fairy

with silken wings

to the flutter of moths

in fine voice sings

While the fairies dance

on the moss below

by the gentle light

of the stars aglow

Wish boxes

Midnight Stars

*"The Midnight Fairy flies across the
early morning sky gathering up the stars."*

Create a large wish box by painting a wood box
and applying small gold stars and glitter.

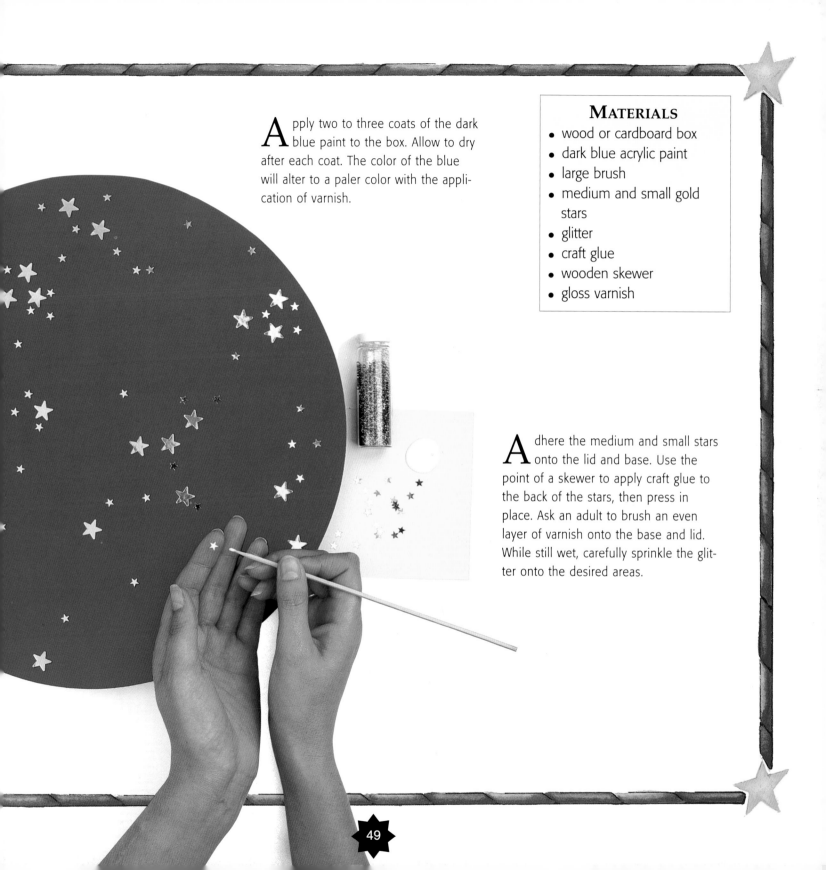

Apply two to three coats of the dark blue paint to the box. Allow to dry after each coat. The color of the blue will alter to a paler color with the application of varnish.

Adhere the medium and small stars onto the lid and base. Use the point of a skewer to apply craft glue to the back of the stars, then press in place. Ask an adult to brush an even layer of varnish onto the base and lid. While still wet, carefully sprinkle the glitter onto the desired areas.

Glimmer Wings

"The Midnight Fairy's special friend is a magical moth whose wings have a golden trim."

A simple folded box can be made to look extra special by cutting it out of gold cardboard and adding glitter and small gold stars.

MATERIALS

- paper
- adhesive tape
- scissors
- colored cardboard
- pencil
- ruler
- craft glue
- glitter
- small stars

Tape the traced pattern to the carbon paper and use a ruler and pen to transfer to the cardboard.

Lightly score the shorter dotted lines. To decorate the box, smear glue over the desired areas, sprinkle on the glitter, and press on the stars.
When the decoration is dry fold the box into shape. Apply glue to the tabs and hold firmly until secure.
Close the box by slotting the wings together.

Trace this half-pattern onto a piece of paper, turn 180 degrees (with the long dotted line being the center), and trace again to achieve the entire box shape. Make sure the cuts at the base of the wings are on the opposite edges of each end, otherwise they will not slide together on the final box. Tape the paper template to cardboard and cut around.

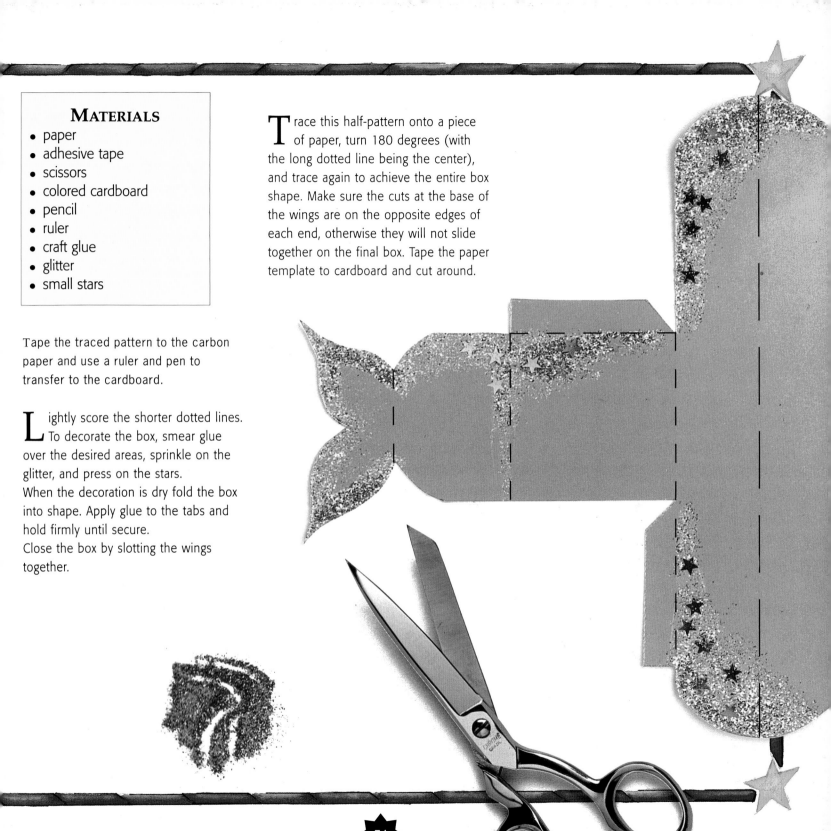

Fairy Wings

"When fairies dance they flutter their wings in midair."

Simply paint a box then attach
the easily made glittering wings.

MATERIALS

- box
- paint: dark blue, mauve
- brush
- coated wire
- pale colored pantyhose
- scissors
- florist's wire
- dimensional glitter paint
- craft glue
- glitter

Apply two or three coats of blue, allowing to dry after each, onto the base and lid.

Prepare the wings by making four oval shapes with the wire, leaving about 1⅝ in (4cm) protruding from each. Make two each of the shapes shown here.

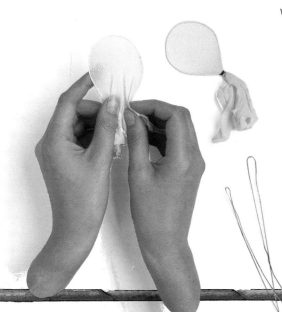

To cover each shape cut a piece of pantyhose 8 x 4 in (20cm 10cm). Pull over the wire as shown and secure with florist's wire. Twist the protruding wires together to connect all four covered shapes into a pair of wings. Add water to the mauve paint until it has a watery consistency. Brush over the entire area of each wing. Add water to the blue paint also and brush over the central portions of each wing. Squeeze a little glitter paint onto your palette and water down, brush over the wing areas. Apply glitter paint directly from the bottle around the edge of each wing. Wrap a small piece of pantyhose around the central wire and paint blue. Poke a hole through the center of the lid. Push the wire ends through the hole and apply a generous amount of glue around the wire on the underneath of the lid.

Midnight Fairy

"When the night is almost over...Starshine begins to sing."

Combine folk art and découpage to show the beauty of the Midnight Fairy.

MATERIALS

- oval-shaped box
- Midnight Fairy print*
- small manicure scissors
- water-based sealer
- paint brushes
  (various widths)
- sponge
- tracing paper
- pencil
- carbon paper
- paints: white, light green,
  dark green, black, purple,
  light purple, medium blue,
  mauve, light blue, tan,
  burgundy, light burgundy,
- water-based gloss varnish

There is a Midnight Fairy print in the back of this book, starting on *page 141. This is intended for use in the Paper Tole project. Make a copy of that print for this box. The publisher grants permission for the print to be reproduced if intended only for personal use, not in the pursuit of income.

Ask an adult to help you carefully cut out the entire Midnight Fairy print. Glue the image to the box lid. Center and gently rub over the image to remove excess glue and air bubbles from underneath. Allow to dry completely.

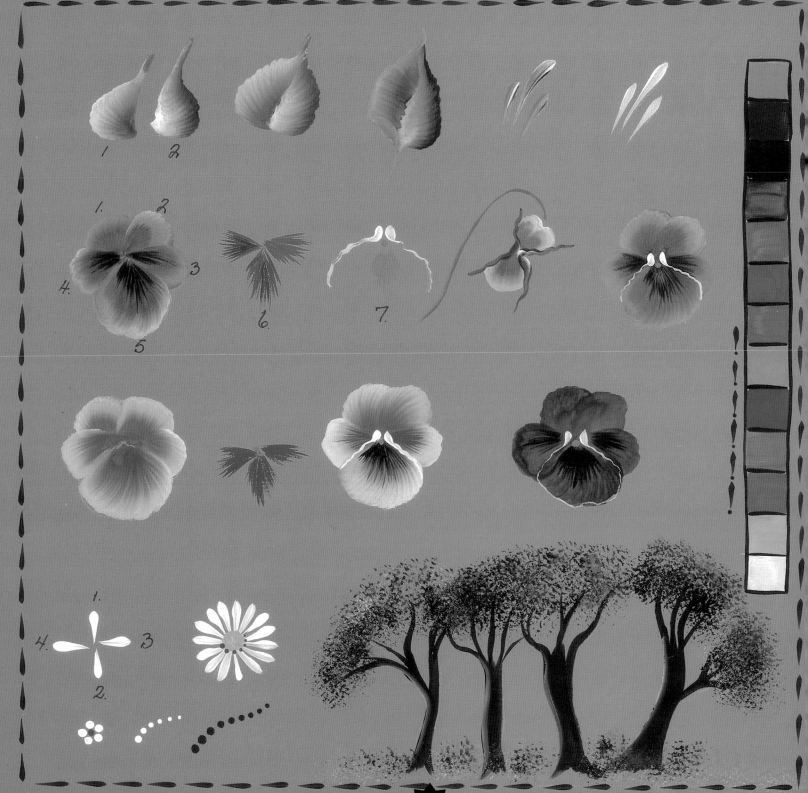

Brush on four or five coats of white paint up to the edge of the image. This is to build the three-dimensonal effect between the image and the paint. As you near the same "level" apply the purple in varying darkness with a sponge. Trace the pattern above and transfer to the lid, using carbon paper. Repeating the pattern until the oval is complete.

Follow the worksheet opposite to paint the box.
Leaves. Combine green and white to create depth in the leaves. Add a little burgundy on the dark green side to achieve shading on some of the leaves.
Pansies. Use the flat brush to paint the pansies. Paint them in a variety of color combinations.

Daisies. Paint the daisies using a round brush and white and yellow paint. Undercoat the side of the box with black. Applying the paint horizontally, shade from the bottom to the top, starting with light blue and gradually adding more purple until the color is completely purple.
Sketch the tree outlines around the box and paint the trunks with the round brush and black and white paint. Sponge the leaves on in black then highlight in places with white.
Ask an adult to finish off the box by applying smooth even coats of varnish.

Preparing for the party

Planning the Party

The magic of the Midnight Fairy turns an ordinary party into a special day that will be remembered forever.

The Midnight Fairy theme of gold, blue, and stars is applied to every aspect of the party day: outfits, room decorations, food, activities, games, and party prizes.

The Midnight Fairy Party is more than just a party; it is an opportunity for everyone to plan and prepare an exciting party day together. Many varied crafts have been included so you can also enjoy the satisfaction of knowing that you have saved money and created unique items.

Involve the whole family in making the craft items. Allowing them to be part of the preparations adds to their feeling of anticipation for the special occasion.

There are some great opportunities for costumes. The Midnight Fairy costume has a flowing skirt, floral headband, and beautiful wings that are easy to make. The Midnight Wizard costume has a star-covered cape and a magical hat.

The first thing to do, three to four weeks in advance, is create a guest list. Determine how many children you want to invite; six is a controllable number. With the help of the party child, make the invitations (page 72), and send them to the intended guests. As children often lose their RSVPs, it's a good idea to include your telephone number so their parents can telephone you direct with their response. When the parents telephone you can suggest that they dress their children in special "fairy" clothes on the party day.

Keep a list of the children you invite and record the responses. If any do not respond, ask the party child to obtain their friends' home numbers and call the parents yourself, so you can be sure how many you are expecting.

It is best to make the party outfits two weeks in advance. However, you will have to resist the pressure from the party child to wear their costume ahead of time!

Party games, prizes, and activities should be planned and prepared a week in advance. Many of these can be done with the help of the party child. Some will need close supervision, while others are quite safe and easy. Read through all of the projects and suggestions first and decide exactly what you wish to include on the party day. You can use all of them, or select only a few if you wish to have a shorter party.

Some of the food can be prepared a day in advance. The sponge cakes can be made either weeks in advance and frozen, or on the day before and stored in an airtight container until ready to be decorated (page 92).

Plan on a 2½-hour party. This will give you time in the morning to decorate the room and table, finish preparing the food, and take care of last-minute details. Read through the decorating suggestions in advance, and purchase the required items so you have them all on hand on the day. Again, employ the help of the family when decorating. This will keep their minds and

hands occupied during the morning of the party, a time when they can become really quite anxious and excited.

Use the blue, gold, and stars to create stunning yet simple accessories and decorations (page 84) that will enhance the magic and excitement of the Midnight Fairy theme. Tie a bunch of gold and blue ribbons and balloons together and attach them to the front gate to identify the party's location.

Read through the party games and activities again and prepare any props or re-arrange any furniture that could be in the way. The more room children have to move in the less likely they are to

knock anything over. Hide the stars for the Star Hunt in the morning, making sure there are no "witnesses".

When the time for the party comes you should have all of the decorations in place, the food prepared, the game props and the party prizes made, and the supplies for the activities close at hand.

The order in which you run the games, activities, and food is entirely up to you, but it is a good idea to plan the party events in advance and commit them to paper so that you can refer to it throughout the party. It is also a good idea to have another adult helper on hand throughout the day to help prepare the food and organize the party games.

A suggestion for a successful running order is:
- When the guests arrive they can join in the simple Coloring-In activity. Have plenty of spare copies* in case some children wish to do more than one.
- After all of the children have arrived they can choose and prepare their Wands.
- To distract them from wanting to play with their "wet" wands, send them outside for a Star Hunt.
- Call the children in from outside and ask them to wash their hands; they've probably been rummaging in the backyard! Invite them to sit down quietly after all their excitement.
- Now they have caught their breath and have clean hands allow them to have their fairy feast, keeping the cake until a little later on.
- Fairy Statues can be played while the food table is cleared and prepared for the Glimmer Toy activity.
- Have each child make a Glimmer Toy, then they can run around the yard, flapping them madly and drying them at the same time.
- Next play a few games:
- Pin the Star on the Wand;
- Fairy Race;
- Musical Toadstools;
- Bring out the Fairy Star Cake next and the children can sing Happy Birthday. Give each child a piece now, and wrap a piece for them to take home in their Cake Basket.
- While the children are digesting their cake they can play Pass The Parcel.

•Finish the party off with Sleeping Fairies.
•While the children are participating in Sleeping Fairies collect their prizes, activities, and party cake so they are ready to go home when their parents arrive.

The games and activities have been combined to offer a mixture of rowdy and quiet pursuits. The children should not be all wound up before they eat, nor run around too wild afterward. It is also a good idea to have quiet game towards the end of the party so that the parents do not arrive to find a screaming mass of excited children.

Through planning the party the children and the activities will be more controlled, and you will not find yourself standing with your hands on your hips demanding that they "quiet down". The fun and enjoyment of The Midnight Fairy Party will make a memorable day for everybody.

* The Publisher grants permission for the Color-In outline and invitation details to be photocopied for purposes relating to the Midnight Fairy Party. Please note it is illegal to use any of the patterns or artwork in this book in the pursuit of income.

The Invitations

Create attractive invitations to send
out to the party guests. Sheets of colored card can be
quickly and easily transformed into either a wizard's hat
or moth's wings. Inside, the invitation details
are photocopied, completed, and glued in place.
For this project you can enlist the help of
the party child. Let them color the
invitations with colored pencils and fill in
the party details while you cut and glue.

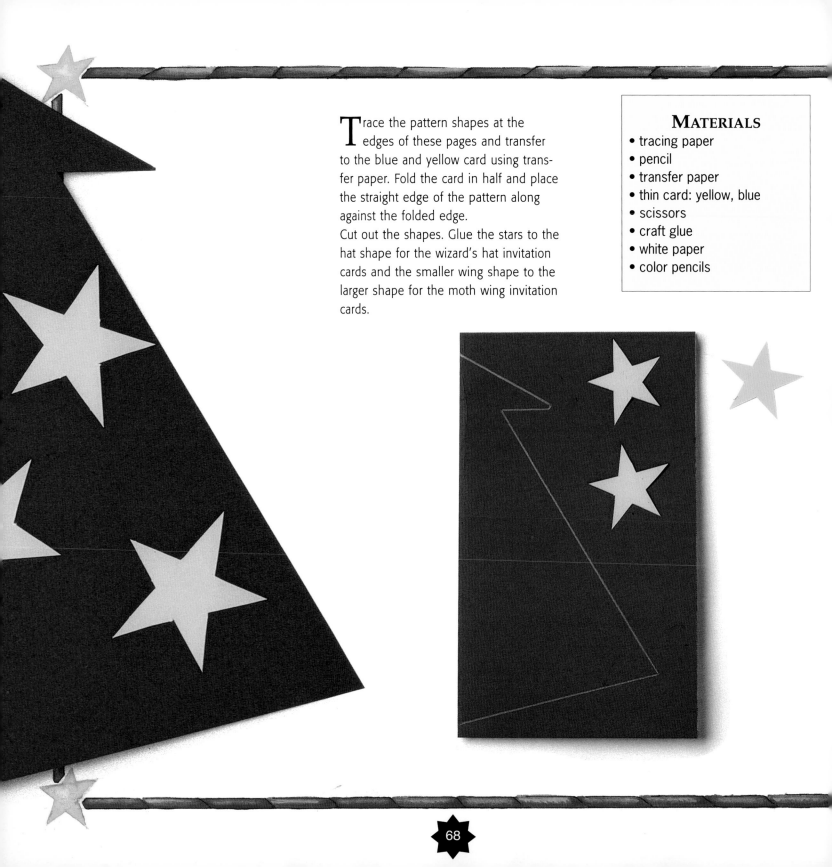

Trace the pattern shapes at the edges of these pages and transfer to the blue and yellow card using transfer paper. Fold the card in half and place the straight edge of the pattern along against the folded edge.

Cut out the shapes. Glue the stars to the hat shape for the wizard's hat invitation cards and the smaller wing shape to the larger shape for the moth wing invitation cards.

MATERIALS

- tracing paper
- pencil
- transfer paper
- thin card: yellow, blue
- scissors
- craft glue
- white paper
- color pencils

To vary the invitations you can use different colored cards.

*You are invited
to a
Midnight Fairy
Birthday Party*

Dear _____

*Please come to my party
I will be* ___ *years old.*

Date _____
Time _____
Place _____
_____

RSVP: by _____ *telephone:* _____

Photocopy the invitation details on the opposite page and cut out along the dotted line. The details will fit onto either of the invitation shapes. Use color pencils to color the stars and add any other decoration you wish. Fill in the details of the party. Position the completed invitation details onto the inside of the cards and glue in place.

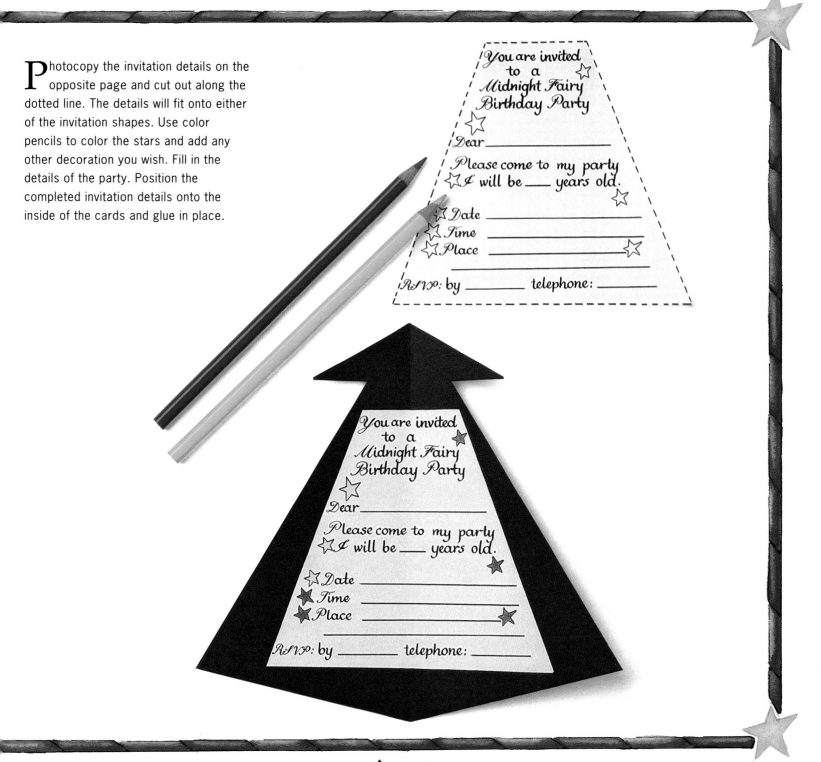

You are invited
to a
Midnight Fairy
Birthday Party

Dear _____

Please come to my party
I will be ___ years old.

Date _____
Time _____
Place _____
_____

RSVP: by _____ telephone: _____

You are invited
to a
Midnight Fairy
Birthday Party

Dear _____

Please come to my party
I will be ___ years old.

Date _____
Time _____
Place _____
_____

RSVP: by _____ telephone: _____

The Outfits

To really capture the magic of the Midnight Fairy
on the party day, the party child will need to be dressed
in a Midnight Fairy outfit. The Midnight Fairy
can wear a flowing fairy skirt made simply from squares
of organza, a decorated headband, starry slippers,
and beautiful painted wings made from
pantyhose and wire. A wizard can wear a wizard's
cape and hat decorated with shiny stars over
blue or black clothes.

MATERIALS
- 47 in (120cm) lengths of organza: white, pale blue, dark blue
- gold thread
- star-shaped sequins
- 4 in (10cm) of interfacing
- pins
- hook and loop fastener
- gold stringed-sequins

Cut approximately eight 13¾ x 13¾ in (35 x 35cm) squares from each of the lengths of organza. The amount you need depends on the length of the waistband (measure the child's waist and add 1⅛ in (3cm), the squares are placed every 1⅛ in (3cm). Using gold thread machine stitch a rolled hem around each square. Hand stitch small star-shaped sequins randomly over each square.

Lay each square of hemmed organza out flat, fold the two opposite corners in and press firmly to create folds. Leave aside.

To make the waistband measure the child's waist. Add 1⅛ in (3cm) and cut a piece of dark blue organza to this length and 3¼ in (8cm) wide. Cut a piece of interfacing to the same measurements. Fold the interfacing in half lengthwise and press. Align the raw edges of the interfacing along one long edge of the organza and pin to hold. Lay interfacing-side down, and begin pinning the points of the organza squares along the waistband evenly, alternating the three colors. Machine stitch to hold.

Fold the waist band in half, wrong sides together, with ⅜ in (10mm) hems, fold in the ends, pin, and machine stitch. Sew a small hook and loop fastener to the ends of the waistband.

The child can wear either a blue t-shirt or a leotard under the skirt. To make the outfit look like the Midnight Fairy's you can add gold stringed-sequins around the shoulder. Hand stitch in place, leaving a loop that lies around the top of the arm.

MATERIALS
- white slippers
- craft glue
- gold stars
- gold glitter paint
- paint brush
- blue ribbon

Glue the gold stars randomly over the slippers. Brush the gold glitter paint around the elastic edge. Tie a small blue bow and glue at the center front of each slipper.

MATERIALS

- assorted silk flowers and leaves
- 5 in (13cm) of covered wire
- craft glue
- dark blue fabric-covered headband

Make this attractive head piece to finish off the outfit. Easily made from a plain headband and silk wired flowers.

Run a thick line of glue along the underside of the silk flowers and covered wire. Press the flowers firmly onto the top of the headband and hold until the glue is secure.

Wire the silk flowers and leaves onto the covered wire, alternating the colors in an attractive sequence.

U ntwist the ends of the four coat hangers and straighten as much as possible. Cut the twisted hook section off two of them with wire cutters; these are for the smaller lower wings. Only an adult should use the wire cutters. Shape the coat hangers like the shapes shown; twist the ends together to hold.
Cut the legs off each pair of pantyhose and stretch over the wire frames. Tie off at bottom to secure.

P aint each wing purple, using the acrylic paint slightly watered down to get good coverage. When dry, paint a white oval onto each wing then a blue outline. Brush the gold glitter paint around the edges of each wing and into the center of the white ovals. Allow to dry. Turn the wings over and paint the other side also if necessary.

Twist the four ends together, securing the wings in the correct position. Wrap the wadding (batting) around the twisted ends to form a padded section. Wrap a length of discarded pantyhose around the padded section. Paint purple. Measure the amount of elastic needed by placing around the child's arm and measuring to the center back. Stitch two loops of elastic to the padded section.

The wizard's cape is a simple design to make using a large half circle of fabric that is then decorated with gold fabric stars and gold glitter paint.

MATERIALS
- 3 ¼ yd (3m) of dark blue fabric
- dressmaker's chalk
- 4 in (10cm) length of wadding (batting)
- iron-on interfacing
- lamé
- double-sided paper-backed fusing
- gold glitter paint

Cut an 82 in (210cm) length from the blue fabric and fold in half lengthwise. Measure 3½ in (9cm) down the folded edge and mark with chalk. Keeping the end of the tape on the same spot, repeat this distance across the fabric in a half circle. Measuring from the same point, measure and mark a second half circle 37 in (95cm) down the fabric. Cut out along these two lines.

Cut 4 in (10cm) wide bias strips and join the short ends together to create a length of bias fabric long enough to go around the curved edge of the cape. Position and pin the bias fabric strip, right sides together, to the lower edge of the cape and machine stitch. Turn the cape wrong side up and fold over the bias fabric to the wrong side, encasing a 4 in (10cm) wide length of wadding (batting), turn under a ⅜ in (10mm) hem and pin in place. Machine stitch along the original stitching line to secure the bottom edge of the cape.

The stand up collar of the Wizard's cape is made with a simple yet effective technique

For the collar cut a 15½ x 4 in (40 x 10cm) piece of blue and a 15½ x 2 in (40 x 5cm) piece of interfacing. Iron the interfacing to the wrong side of the fabric aligning along one long edge. Pin to the neck edge of the cape right sides together. Machine stitch.

Cut two 12 x 1⅝ in (30 x 4cm) lengths of blue and fold wrong sides together lengthwise. Stitch along three sides and turn right side out. Press.

Fold the collar to the wrong side and fold in ⅜ in (10mm) hems on all three sides. Insert the ties at each end and pin. Pin the entire collar in place and stitch along the three sides.

Cut star shapes, using the pattern opposite, from lamé fabric and apply to the cape using double-sided paper-backed fusing. Apply a line of gold glitter paint around the star shapes and allow to dry.

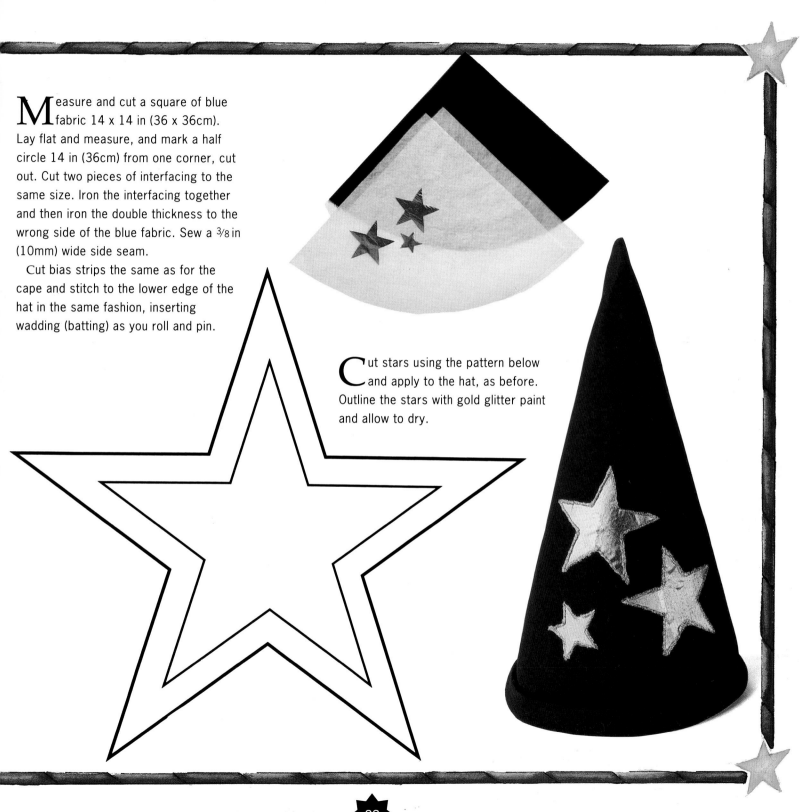

Measure and cut a square of blue fabric 14 x 14 in (36 x 36cm). Lay flat and measure, and mark a half circle 14 in (36cm) from one corner, cut out. Cut two pieces of interfacing to the same size. Iron the interfacing together and then iron the double thickness to the wrong side of the blue fabric. Sew a 3/8 in (10mm) wide side seam.

Cut bias strips the same as for the cape and stitch to the lower edge of the hat in the same fashion, inserting wadding (batting) as you roll and pin.

Cut stars using the pattern below and apply to the hat, as before. Outline the stars with gold glitter paint and allow to dry.

Decorating the Room

Decorate the main party room with the gold, yellow, and blue color scheme. You can enhance the enchanted atmosphere if you purchase glistening gold and clear balloons and shimmering curling ribbon and attach these around the walls and bunched up in the corners. They even look nice in piles on the floor. Cut out star, moon, and moth wing shapes to suspend from the ceiling and drape blue and yellow crepe ribbons from corner to corner.

85

Using these shapes as patterns trace and cut out as many star, moon, and moth-wing shapes as you need to fill the party room.

Poke a small hole at the top of each shape and attach a length of fishing line.

MATERIALS
- gold cardboard
- tracing paper
- pencil
- transfer paper
- scissors
- fishing line or yarn

To suspend the shapes you can attach a long length of fishing line (or yarn) from one curtain rod to another on the other side of the room. If you do not have curtain rods you could push small thumb tacks into the top of door frames instead. Tie the shapes to the lines at varying heights. Keep in mind the size of the children and hang to suit, but not too low or they will be grabbed at and everything will come down!

MATERIALS
- curling ribbons: blue, gold
- scissors

Holding the blades of the scissors open run the curling ribbon across the edge of the blade using your thumb to hold the ribbon taught.
Tie the curled ribbons into small bunches then either tie onto the balloons or use individually to decorate the room.

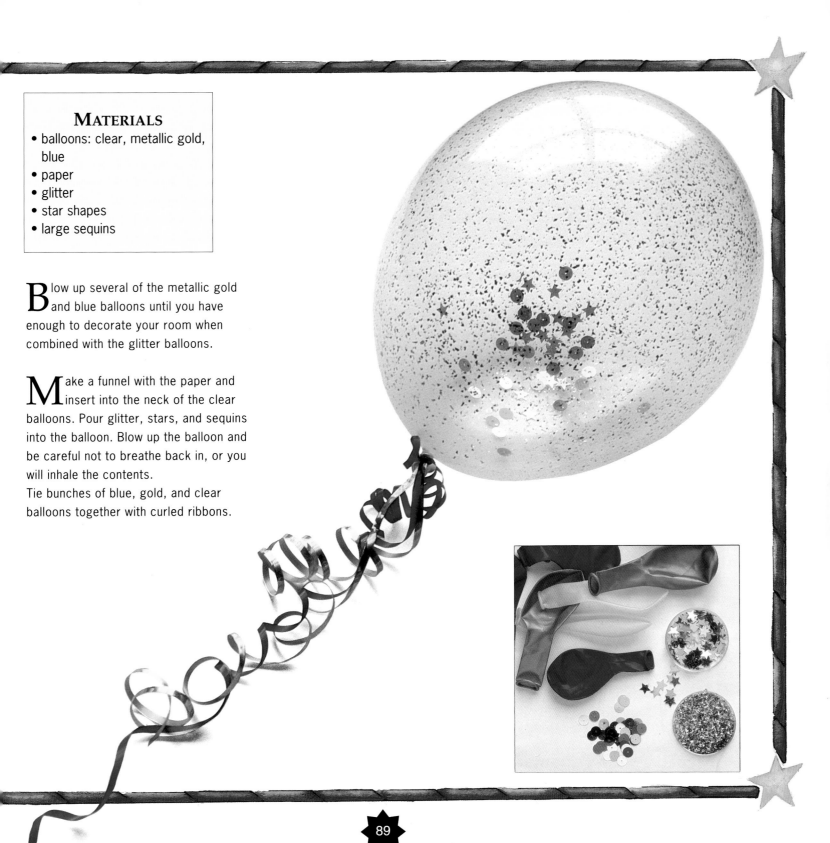

MATERIALS

- balloons: clear, metallic gold, blue
- paper
- glitter
- star shapes
- large sequins

Blow up several of the metallic gold and blue balloons until you have enough to decorate your room when combined with the glitter balloons.

Make a funnel with the paper and insert into the neck of the clear balloons. Pour glitter, stars, and sequins into the balloon. Blow up the balloon and be careful not to breathe back in, or you will inhale the contents.
Tie bunches of blue, gold, and clear balloons together with curled ribbons.

Food & table decorations

91

Cakes

Home-made sponge mixes can be easily made into a large star-shaped cake and small fairy cakes that will delight all of the children at the party.

- 2 round chocolate sponges,
  8 in (20cm) in diameter
  (see p.138)
- icing: chocolate, vanilla
  (see p.139)
- knife
- gold and silver edible balls
- colored sprinkles
- piping bag
- sparklers

Cut one of the chocolate sponges into six equal sections by cutting across the center first then measure 4 in (10cm) around the side to find the correct place for the next two cuts.

Trim off the round edges as indicated in the picture below. Without cutting the second cake, mark the surface with the same divisions and then trim off the round edges to give six flat sides.

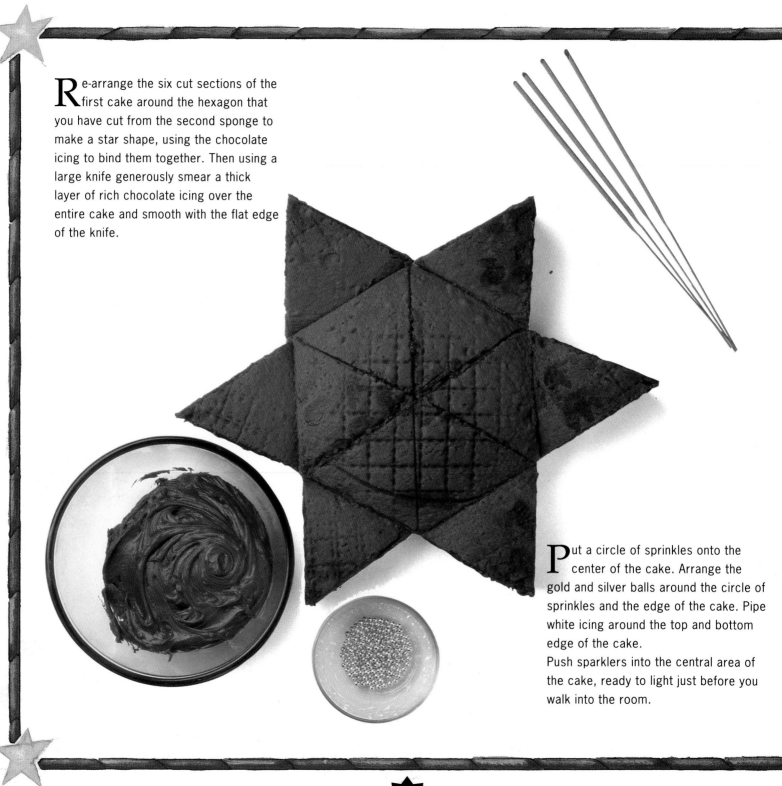

Re-arrange the six cut sections of the first cake around the hexagon that you have cut from the second sponge to make a star shape, using the chocolate icing to bind them together. Then using a large knife generously smear a thick layer of rich chocolate icing over the entire cake and smooth with the flat edge of the knife.

Put a circle of sprinkles onto the center of the cake. Arrange the gold and silver balls around the circle of sprinkles and the edge of the cake. Pipe white icing around the top and bottom edge of the cake.
Push sparklers into the central area of the cake, ready to light just before you walk into the room.

Using a sharp knife slice the top off each cup cake. Cut the top into two equal pieces. Spread icing over the bottom half of the cup cake and push the two top pieces into the icing so they look like wings. Put more icing between the wings to make the moth's body.

Use two edible colored balls as eyes and for color put sprinkles over the body section. As a finishing touch you can push thin strips of chocolate into the icing as antennae.

Drink, Bread and Crackles

The food and drink at the Midnight Fairy Party should be the sorts of things that children will think fairies really do eat when they have their parties.

MATERIALS

- chocolate crackles (see p. 139)
- colored edible balls
- sliced white bread
- butter
- colored sprinkles
- lemonade
- blue food coloring

For a special drink at the Midnight Fairy Party you can make Dream Nectar. This is made by simply adding a few drops of blue food coloring to lemonade to make it turn blue.

Chocolate Crackles are quick and easy to make (see page 139) for parties and are always a favorite with children. Decorate them with colored balls, and put them in silver party cake cups to make them look sparkly.

To prepare the Fairy Bread take slices of bread and spread on butter right to the edges. Cut off the crusts and shake colored sprinkles evenly over the bread. Cut each piece into four triangles and arrange on gold trimmed plates.

Tablecloth and Napkins

Paper tablecloths and napkins can be purchased from supermarkets for very little outlay. Plain white tablecloths can be stamped with star shapes in the blue and gold color theme and the napkins are rolled into fun spirals.

MATERIALS
- paper
- kitchen sponge
- scissors
- white paper tablecloth
- acrylic paint: blue, gold

Trace the star pattern onto white paper and cut out. Using this as a template, cut a star shape from the sponge. Lightly dip the sponge star into the paint and coat evenly; stamp onto the tablecloth around the edges.

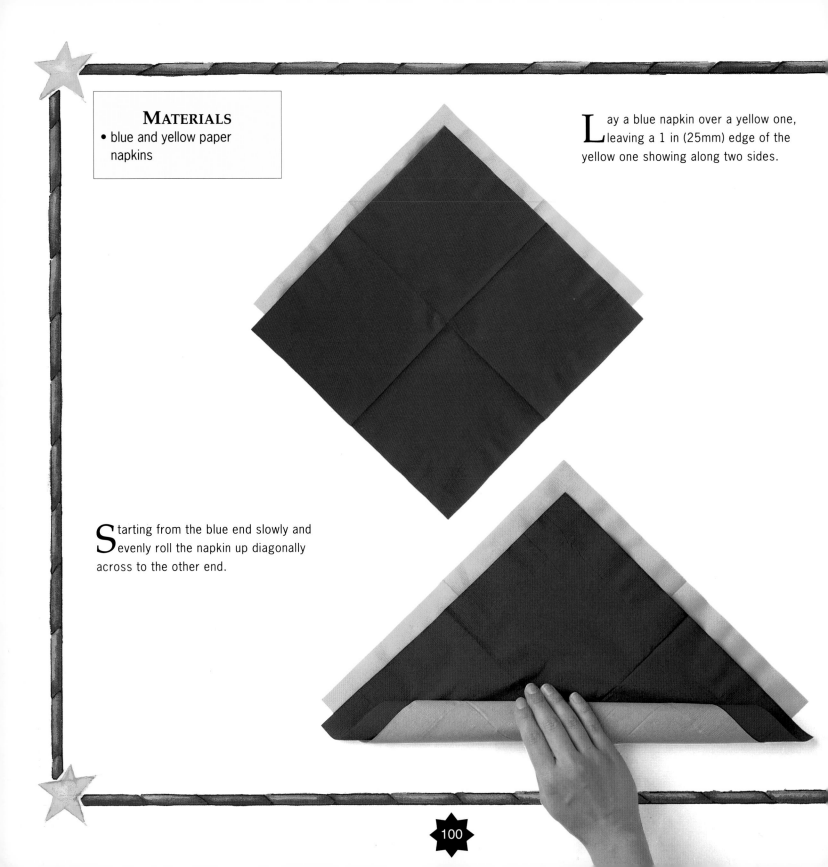

Lay a blue napkin over a yellow one, leaving a 1 in (25mm) edge of the yellow one showing along two sides.

Starting from the blue end slowly and evenly roll the napkin up diagonally across to the other end.

As you roll past the half way mark the stripes will begin to form along the napkin roll. When complete pinch to hold in the center.

The rolled napkins are then folded in half. They will hold their folded shape if laid flat on the table, but they look better if they are stood in plastic cups. Place one cup and napkin at each setting on your party table.

Cups, Plates and Place Cards

The food and drink utensils can be brightened up to fit in the Midnight Fairy theme by the quick and easy application of sticky star shapes. The place cards are simply photocopied, colored, and folded to mark each child's place at the party table. These projects can be safely undertaken by the family in advance of the party.

MATERIALS

- clear plastic cups
- blue plastic plates
- sticky star shapes

To create cups that fit in with the Midnight Fairy theme, randomly apply lots of small sticky stars to the outside of clear plastic cups. Combined with colorful drinks this makes an interesting feature on the party table.

To decorate party plates in a matching style, apply the sticky stars to the very outside rim of the plates only, avoiding the food area.

103

Photocopy the place card outline onto the yellow paper and color in the Midnight Fairy with crayons. Write each child's name in the space provided.

C ut out the outside rectangle of the place card. Then using the craft knife carefully cut along the outline of the Midnight Fairy's wings and head that are above the dotted fold line only. A craft knife must only be used by adults.

F old the back of the card down carefully along the dotted fold line, making sure not to fold over the Midnight Fairy. On the day of the party place the cards where each child is to sit.

Games & activities

Wands

One way to keep children entertained at parties is to give them a craft activity to do. These wands will not only keep them busy, they will provide a Midnight Fairy Party keepsake that can be taken home.

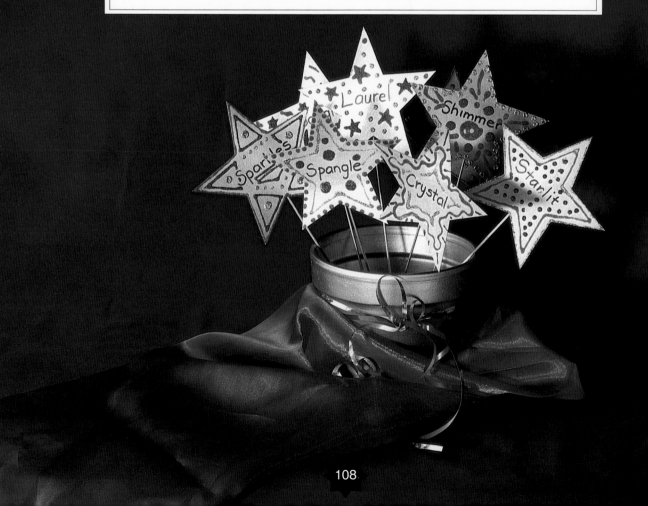

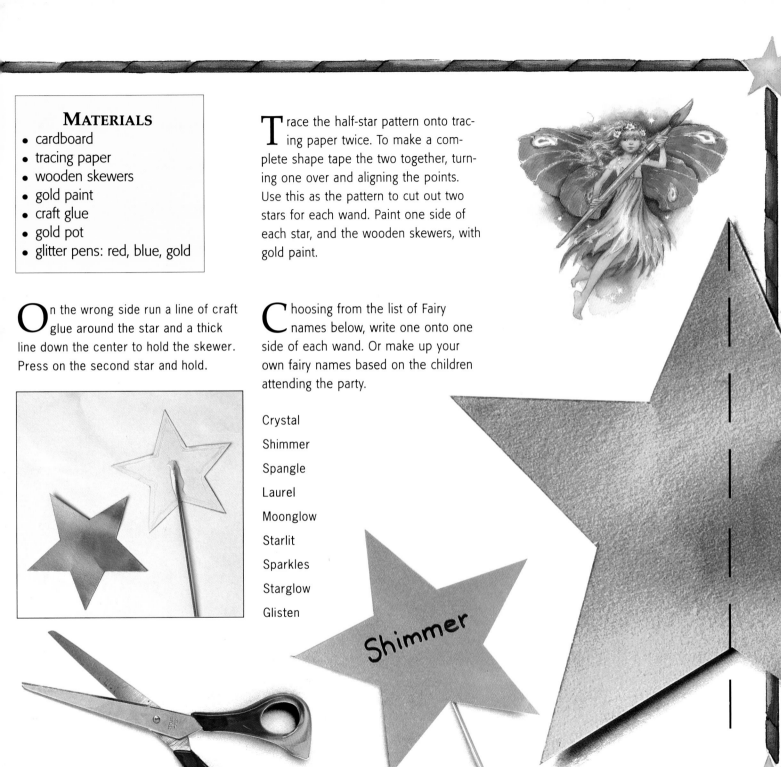

MATERIALS
- cardboard
- tracing paper
- wooden skewers
- gold paint
- craft glue
- gold pot
- glitter pens: red, blue, gold

Trace the half-star pattern onto tracing paper twice. To make a complete shape tape the two together, turning one over and aligning the points. Use this as the pattern to cut out two stars for each wand. Paint one side of each star, and the wooden skewers, with gold paint.

On the wrong side run a line of craft glue around the star and a thick line down the center to hold the skewer. Press on the second star and hold.

Choosing from the list of Fairy names below, write one onto one side of each wand. Or make up your own fairy names based on the children attending the party.

Crystal

Shimmer

Spangle

Laurel

Moonglow

Starlit

Sparkles

Starglow

Glisten

Shimmer

On the day of the party take the partially prepared wands and arrange them in a gold sprayed terracotta plant pot that you have made ready by putting sand inside to hold them in place. When arranged use as a table centerpiece until it is time for the children to decorate them.

To prepare for the activity cover a table with newspaper, place the pot with the wands in the center and scatter the glitter pens around.

Allow each child to choose a wand with the name on it that they would like to have for the day. Encourage the children to decorate their wands with swirls, blobs, lines, and stars.

When they have finished applying the paint, carefully arrange the wands back into the pot to dry before they play with them.

Coloring-in

As the children wait for all the guests to arrive, they can color in photocopies of the Midnight Fairy herself; again, they can take them home as keepsakes.

A few days in advance of the party you can photocopy the artwork on this page. To make it fit on a standard piece of writing paper you should enlarge it by 175%.

E ncourage the children to color their pictures at a time when you need them to settle down from the excitement.

Glimmer Toy

*Cut out the moth wings in advance of the party
and supply one to each child to make and take home.*

glimmer wings pattern

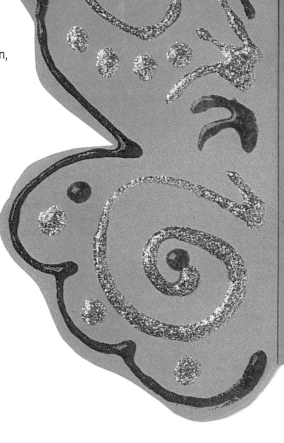

Trace the pattern shape and cut out from colored paper as many pairs of Glimmer moth-wings as needed in advance of the party.

Supply the children with a moth-wing shape each and encourage them to decorate it with the glitter pens. After the paint dries, lightly score along the fold lines and fold the wings back to create a channel to glue the stick into. Wrap and glue paper around the part of the stick that will be the body of the moth. Glue in place. If the child holds the end of the stick and waves the moth up and down, the wings will flap.

Fairy Statues

Fairy Statues is an active game that should be played in a large room free of fragile items that could be broken as the children dance about. Alternatively it could be played outside.

To play the game all of the children dance about the room to music and when the music stops they must strike a statue pose and not move or giggle. Any child that moves is out.

Resume the music and the remaining children dance again until you stop the music again. Continue dancing and posing like statues until the winner is the only one left that hasn't moved.

To make the game more fairy like, suggest that the children strike poses like fairies and wizards would and choose music that has a "magical" sound, such as flutes, bells, or a xylophone.

Pin the Star on the Wand

U se a photocopier to enlarge the outline of the Midnight Fairy on page 113 onto large paper and let the party child color it in ready for the party.

O n the day of the party tape the colored picture onto a surface that cannot be damaged, such as the fridge or on an outside wall.

Each child is blindfolded with a scarf or strip of fabric and given a small gold cardboard star shape with a piece of adhesive tape on the back.

Stand the child in front of the picture and spin around a few times so they forget where the wand is. Face them in the direction of the picture and tell them to attach the star to where they think the end of the Midnight Fairy's wand is. Use a pen to mark where the star is positioned and then blindfold the next child.

The winner is the child who places their star closest to the end of the wand.

T race the star shape above onto cardboard, cut out, and paint gold. Roll a strip of adhesive tape into a circle and attach to the back of the star so it will adhere to the picture where placed.

Sleeping Fairies

This is a good game to play just before it's time to go home. It gives the children time to relax and slow down.

To play the game all of the children lie on the floor with their eyes closed and they are not allowed to move.

One child is "in" and places candies onto the sleeping fairies faces and bodies. If the sleeping fairies move or giggle they are out.

The tickly feeling of having candies placed on their faces and bodies makes it difficult for the children to resist moving, but they must remain still in order to win the game.

As the children begin to move and are gradually dropped out one by one, you can suggest that they sit quietly, so they do not wake the remaining sleeping fairies.

Star Hunt

This game can be played inside or outside. If it's inside you could run the risk of having your things turned upside down as the children enthusiastically search for the hidden stars. You can tell them that they cannot move things, only look under or around.

If you plan to have six children at the Midnight Fairy party you should make twelve or more stars to hide.

Using the pattern below as a guide, the star shapes are cut and colored in advance of the party and wrapped candy taped to the back of each one.

Hide the stars around the house or yard and invite the children to go on a star hunt. The more stars they find the more candy they get to eat.

Fairy Race

124

This game, unlike the name suggests, is quite a controlled game with no running about but it will require some space to run the race in.

This game is a race that is determined by the numbers that come up on the dice, and the first child to reach the predetermined finishing line is the winner. Using the pattern on the left cut out six star shapes and number each one from 1–6. Using double-sided tape attach one to each child's chest.

Roll the two dice and the children with the stars that correspond to the numbers on the dice are allowed to take one jump forward. Their feet must be together and they must stand on the spot where they land until their number is rolled again. The first child to the finishing line is the winner.

Pass the Parcel

Place a package of candy in the center of the parcel and wrap with layer after layer of colored paper, placing a wish star in every three layers.

Sit the children in a circle and give the parcel to one of them. Start up the music and tell the child holding the parcel to pass it around the circle from one child to the next until the music stops.

The child holding the parcel when the music stops unwraps one sheet from the parcel. If there is nothing in the wrapping they pass it on again when the music resumes; if there is a wish star they close their eyes and make a wish, keeping it secret of course!

Continue passing the parcel until the last layer is unwrapped. The child who unwraps is the winner and keeps the package of candy.

Cut out three or four star shapes from some gold card, using the star above as a pattern. Write the words "Make A Wish" on each one ready to insert in the layers of the parcel.

make a WISH

Musical Toadstools

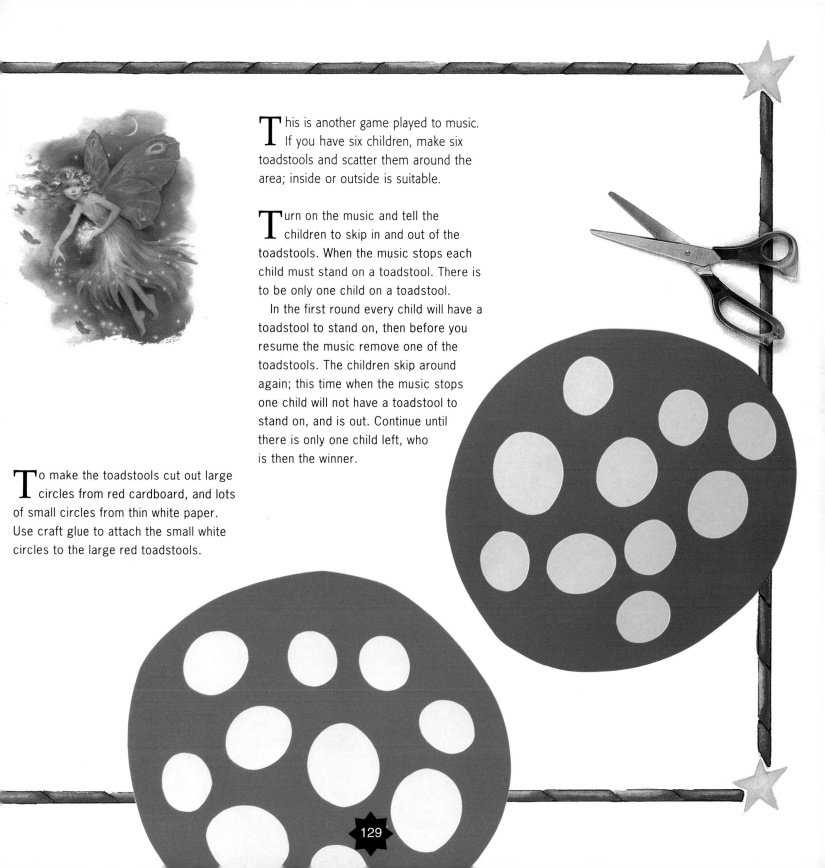

This is another game played to music. If you have six children, make six toadstools and scatter them around the area; inside or outside is suitable.

Turn on the music and tell the children to skip in and out of the toadstools. When the music stops each child must stand on a toadstool. There is to be only one child on a toadstool.

In the first round every child will have a toadstool to stand on, then before you resume the music remove one of the toadstools. The children skip around again; this time when the music stops one child will not have a toadstool to stand on, and is out. Continue until there is only one child left, who is then the winner.

To make the toadstools cut out large circles from red cardboard, and lots of small circles from thin white paper. Use craft glue to attach the small white circles to the large red toadstools.

Wish bag

When the party games are played you need prizes to give the winners. The prizes can be things as easy as candy or a small package of coloring pencils or something more special like this Wish Bag. It will not take very long to make up six or so in advance of the party day. When handing out the prizes be sure to have a different winner each time so that the special prizes are equally distributed.

MATERIALS

- 8 in (20cm) light blue satin
- 1 in (2.5cm) wide lace ribbon: light blue, white
- Gold embroidery thread
- safety pin
- iron-on interfacing

C ut out a piece of satin 4¾ x 8¼ in (12 x 21cm). Turn down a ¼ in (10mm) hem twice, toward the wrong side. Press and stitch along the fold. Cut a piece of lace to the same length as the folded hemmed edge and machine stitch onto the satin with a zig zag stitch.

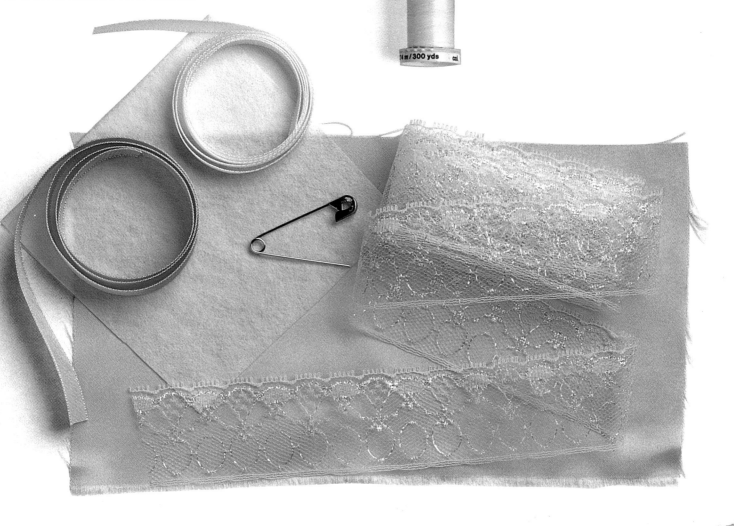

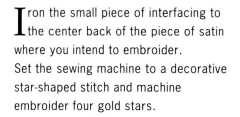

Iron the small piece of interfacing to the center back of the piece of satin where you intend to embroider.
Set the sewing machine to a decorative star-shaped stitch and machine embroider four gold stars.

Place the length of light blue ribbon, onto the right side of the bag, across the top edge of the satin just below the lace. Turn under each raw end and pin in place. Machine stitch along both long edges.

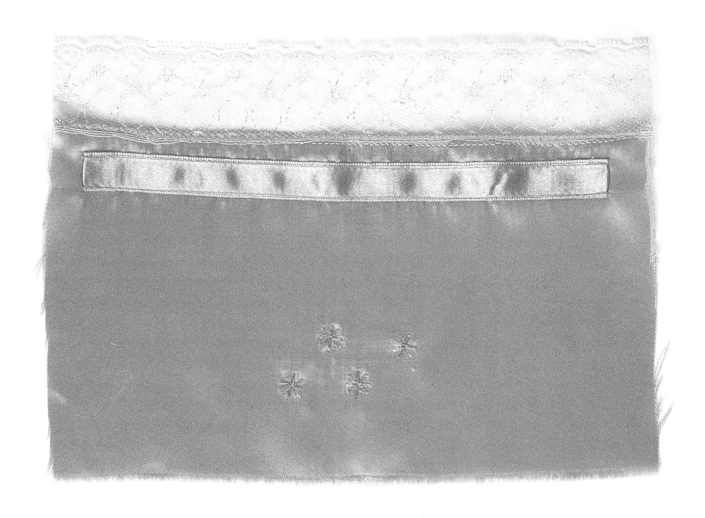

Fold the piece of satin with the right sides together, and the short edges aligned. Machine stitch the length with a 3/8 in (10mm) seam.

Refold the satin so the seam is down the center back and the sides of the bag are on the folds. Machine stitch a seam across the bottom 3/8 in (10mm) from the raw edge. Turn the bag right side out and press with a cool iron.

Place a safety pin in one end of the white ribbon and thread it through the ribbon casing. The opening of the casing is at the back of the bag. When you have completely threaded the white ribbon through cross it over at the back of the wish bag and bring it around to the front and tie into a small bow.

Stars on Pencils

Decorative pencils are always popular with children and
these ones are simple to make. Just glue two gold star shapes
to the end of a pencil and spray gold.

Use the shape below as a pattern and cut two stars for each pencil. Sharpen one end of each pencil; this end will be inserted into the star shapes.

Apply a generous amount of glue to the wrong side of one of the star shapes and put the sharpened end of the pencil onto the star, press the other star on, and hold securely until the glue begins to set. Make as many as needed.

When the glue is set, spray the pencil and star all over with the gold spray paint. Be certain the paint is non-toxic, and do not allow a child to use the spray can without supervision. Allow to dry.

Cake basket

As each child leaves the party wrap a piece of the
Fairy Star Cake in a napkin and place in a shiny gold
Cake Basket to carry home.

MATERIALS

- tracing paper
- pencil
- transfer paper
- gold cardboard
- scissors or craft knife
- stapler

Using a folded piece of tracing paper place the folded edge on the dotted line of the basket pattern. Trace off the shape and transfer to the gold cardboard. Carefully cut out with either a craft knife or scissors. Lightly score the inner lines along the four sides of the base. Gently bend the box sides upward and place a staple in each side to secure. Cut the handle out of gold card and position from one side to the other. Staple to secure.

Wrap small pieces of cake carefully in a paper napkins and put them inside the baskets to give to each child as they leave the party.

basket pattern

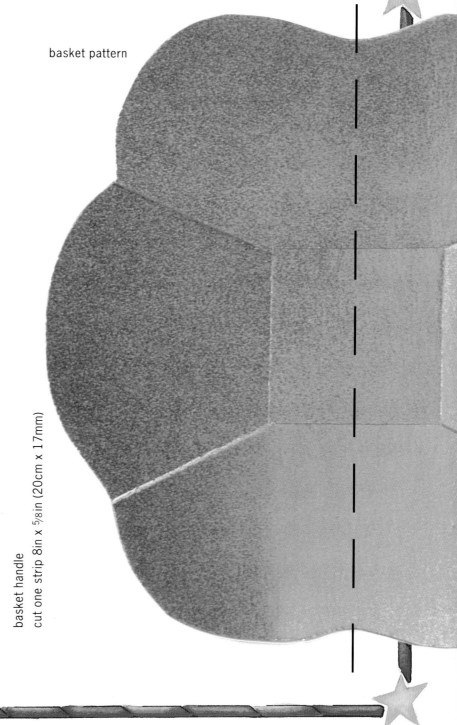

basket handle
cut one strip 8in x ⅝in (20cm x 17mm)

Recipes

Basic Sponge

INGREDIENTS
- 4 oz (100g) margarine
- 4 oz (100g) fine white sugar
- 2 eggs
- 4 oz (100g) self-raising flour
- 1 level tsp baking powder

Mix the ingredients together until they are completely blended. Pour into a greased 8 in (20cm) round cake tin and bake at 350°F (185°C).

Fairy Star Cake - chocolate.

Prepare two basic sponge mixes substituting 1oz (25g) of the flour for 1oz (25g) cocoa. Fill two deep 8in (20cm) cake tins and bake in the oven for approximately 30 minutes.

Fairy Cakes.

Prepare the basic sponge mix and add a few drops of blue food coloring if desired. Spoon the mixture into individual party cake cups. Bake for 15 minutes.

I^{cing}

INGREDIENTS
- 6 oz (175g) soft butter or margarine
- 9 oz (250g) sifted confectioners' sugar
- cocoa powder or vanilla essence
- one or two drops of boiling water

Cream the butter or margarine until soft. Gradually introduce the sifted sugar and mix until smooth and fluffy. If the mixture becomes too stiff, add one or two drops of boiling water to soften. Use two teaspoons of cocoa to make chocolate icing or a few drops of vanilla essence for white vanilla icing.

C^{hocolate Crackles}

INGREDIENTS
- 4 cups of puffed rice cereal
- 9 oz (250g) of margarine or butter, melted and cooled
- 3 Tbsp of cocoa
- 1 cup coconut
- 1½ cups sifted confectioners' sugar

Mix the dry ingredients thoroughly. Make a well in the center; pour in the margarine or butter and mix well. Spoon into party cake cups and refrigerate until set.

Paper Tole Print

On the following page is the Midnight
Fairy print to be photocopied for the
Paper Tole project beginning on
page 34.

INDEX